my name is abilene

Also by Elisabeth Sennitt Clough

ELISABETH SENNITT CLOUGH

my name is abilene

SALT

CROMER

PUBLISHED BY SALT PUBLISHING 2023

2 4 6 8 10 9 7 5 3 1

First published in Great Britain in 2023 by
Salt Publishing Ltd
12 Norwich Road, Cromer, Norfolk NR27 0AX United Kingdom

www.saltpublishing.com

Salt Publishing Limited Reg. No. 5293401

A CIP catalogue record for this book is available from the British Library

ISBN 978 1 78463 281 6 (Paperback edition)

Typeset in Sabon by Salt Publishing

Printed and bound in Great Britain by Clays Ltd, Elcograf S.p.A

to my mother

Contents

before john

abilene

my name is abilene

before john

the autumn i turn sixteen
i riddle maris pipers for 2.50 p/h   *cavort cavort*
at the end of the row i'm the tail
on a spine of older women
who share their wisdom   *cavort cavort*
don't spread manure on potato land
planting during moonlight will scupper a crop
even after harvest potatoes live on   *cavort cavort*
heat and moisture cause them to shoot
this season my belly prickles with love   *cavort cavort*
i've found inside the spinney
all day the belt tumbles along   *cavort cavort*
its dirt settles in my pores
one day you're a child   *cavort cavort*
the next you're carrying one
the split and blotchy potatoes   *cavort cavort*
i toss from the conveyor
land with a half-hearted thud

the box of maternal recall

it arrives on an ordinary wednesday
a plain brown parcel on your mat
you notice its smell
something warm
corpuscular

□

the women in your family
believe rain is like love
there one minute and all over you
then

□

female relatives illustrate
your tarot pack

□

insofar as you use the verb echo
only because you like the final *oh*
how it stays in your mouth

□

you ask your own ghost
for relationship advice

□

all those messages
tied to the ankles of babies

open it, corrugated and sodden with drizzle
a plain brown parcel on your lap
you are becoming used to
the soft damp
rising

□

the primary school excursion
when the rickety stilts beneath the museum-whale were you
and the museum-whale on top of the rickety stilts was you

□

how it's always the same rain

□

the way the women in your family have always played to
    men
who call girls *women* and women *girls*

□

nothing will ever touch your body
the way rain does

□

the knowledge that somewhere there's a better sunset

loosened of its slithery paper and pellets of foam
a plain brown parcel in your hands
find the little being in its folds
milk-fed and swaddled
poor drunk moth

☐

how there's no community
for the women who leave

☐

but if there was
your name would be a euphemism for it

☐

sistren, though you may hate your life
you put your hands and feet inside the ride

☐

how as a child you preferred the box over its shiny contents
because you could fill it with your own imaginings

☐

none of this is your fault

☐

it all is

the village women and my mother

if we breathe the same air does that make us part of one
    other?
        in the beginning she was my mum
clear off and take your bastard wi' you
        she didn't dress like the villagers
she were in that floppy hat again
        they thought she was a townie
even them are living better than us now

then she'd passed the scholarship to high school
        non ducor duco
she didn't pronounce things the same way they did
        the vicar's hosting a boo-fay
she'd moved four miles down the road into their village
        she's not one of us

by and by she didn't react to their slurs
        they ignored her hats, her *boo-fays* and her latin
for like her they knew the wasps' nests that balance
        on the rafters of men's bedrooms

bormed

they stick to me, those wonky-handled years –
nights of chip fat and dripping, a briny stench
of boiling bacon from a two-ring stove,
my blazer pocket damp with sly handfuls
of *you'll sit there 'til you eat it* boiled cabbage.
mum's tongue moving over consonants
in ways us hayseeds never learned, my brothers
insult each other, sail their yellow boat
through cloudy bathwater, take turns
to skipper a safe passage between jetties
of blue band margarine tubs. the water is cold,
time slow. in the front room, mum's wallpaper
wears nicotine stains and patches of damp
on the fleur-de-lys repeat. the decorator's signature,
barry 1986, hides behind the clock in cursive pencil.
this is the world young widowhood created,
codeine bottles and cotton balls beneath her bed,
a nightstand cluttered with bottles of empty scent,
pillows splashed with gin from those times she didn't
steady me for the razor blades and condoms, the guck
and brawn of stepdaddies and uncle-daddies:
come you here, fratchy gow, come you here, their prints
in castrol gtx over the back-kitchen door –
it's been four decades and i'm still bormed
by those years, whining at inattentive gods
to just let a good rain rumble and pour.

paradise farm

don't piss on my leg
and tell me it's raining
the *for sale by auction* sign says *paradise farm*
but i know this is the yard
of the house i grew up in
i'm an adult tourist
in my fen-poor childhood
where the past crunches
beneath me like old cowpats
my sister loretta calls me
says she want her tamworths back
she needs their piggy melodies
to fill her double atcost barn
trust her to stick her snout in
she surfaces from a chicken run
clawed, strawy
a shat-on kinswoman of hens
calls me *ducky*
i tell her to go shave her alpacas
and the fen wind pants
round the concrete floor
and out the doorway
where it worries the asbestos roof

loretta likes to know people

even when she's already made her mind up about them
loretta's the type to dress up for her weekly food shop
she doesn't walk anywhere
drives a car with a roomy boot
a faux-farmer who breeds alpacas
and has re-mortgaged her children's inheritance
for her 4×4, twelve alpacas
and a clutch of young male *friends*

loretta's friends don't have regular jobs
but if they do, they also have a business on the side
these businesses are the equivalent
of miniature ramekins of coleslaw
served next to porterhouse steak
they don't bring much to anyone's life
and may or may not be above board

loretta's friends don't worry about the law
because it only exists in places like cambridge
loretta keeps her windows clean
her thoughts mucky

at night the savage plants sing

good bluesy karaoke
songs in which i could lose my way
then find myself otherwise
in the america of my imagination

it could all end there
the plants, their songs and my hunger
for a recycled emotional experience

but a moth zapped by a café light box
animates their prickly lips
o leaf-miner, o fevered-away dear
the end should never be a kick of neon
trailed by a chorus of dust

my venuses know that the world
needs to caress its prey first
embrace it in cilia-coated lobes
filled with nectar

there have to be stages
before an exoskeleton is snapped
its good marrow siphoned away

﷼

they wear the fabric of their dresses loose
enough for insects to nuzzle inside
to let the bees bully them a little

some years the nectar dries up
and there's nothing but poison
those seasons the wind tears at petals

it's not difficult to understand
how the toxins in foxgloves
that cause sickness and confusion
can also regulate the heart

mum's in her new garden
with its brick path, its beds
of hollyhocks and chinese lanterns
she crouches at the edge of the pond
scans the water for fish
that are already dead
brace's ring slips from her finger
wobbles through the cloudy water
mired with run-off from the tip next door
princess a voice calls *princess*
i will fetch your ring
if you let me lay down with you
on your starched white sheets

in their black soil, the potatoes grow harder, their eyes
unformed and glaucous. in turn no one sees them, no one
knows they are there for months and months. in the after-
state, if they aren't stored properly, they release deadly
nightshade toxins that can kill. but after a life spent in
dirt, all that potatoes want is to be fluffy on the inside

mum's *thinking of yous* and *happy ever afters*
demanded manure and bonemeal
a knees-in-dirt spring taught me
the hunger of roses is meaty
when a flower doesn't bloom
fix the environment in which it grows
not the flower
i think of mum three sheets to the wind
on the back kitchen floor
empty bottles beneath potato peel
brace sat with benny hill and a plate of greasy chips
she'll get up when she's ready he mutters
she's all right there
in front of the fire
i wanted to tell him *i love the compassion in your voice*
on the colour chart it would be peachy pink
the next day mum planted two *together forevers*

＊

some days i want to knife you
in your frilly crimson hearts
it doesn't matter how pretty you look
or how fragrant you smell
your crybaby heads thrive on horse shit

*if one of us forgets to water the flowers and herbs
what will mask the smell of decay?* asks the girl
abilene. everyone mutters the lord's prayer in reverse
and the girl abilene watches a grub writhe on a leaf.
the villagers stand on their doorsteps spit in the
direction of the wind and cross themselves. why worry
about the cows giving blood instead of milk when the
faithful sit under their bridges take instruction from
eels and pike? ague, are we there yet? the girl abilene
is always there for songs and stories and to let you
know your cabbage field's been set alight. the walls
aren't closing in they're falling down. the dykes are
full of boggarts and tiddly muns and lantern men.
and the village folk don't even know which of the
village languages the fish are in. the girl abilene asks
do you ever listen to the dead? hold their dry tongues
in your ears? they'd tell you to run backwards from
the bouquets of posies and herbs. fix yourself in the
direction of the plague-cart

a yard of big dogs

i don't remember being afraid of rabies. tuberculosis. fun-
house mirrors. the fly-littered carcass of a mad cow. thin
air or thick thieves. boggy fields. the witch or her flying
monkeys. elastic dangling from my knickers. spam and
boiled potatoes. the colour brown. upside down pond
fish. frizzy lettuce. the stare of the magpie. any number
of magpies.

but what my mum's friend pete said to me is a four-dog
yard with a flimsy chain-link fence. saliva shining on the
gravel. the dogs drooling over their first bite of my ten-
year-old body as i struggle to outrun their wet mouths.

a woman on a blue bike stops to take a picture of mum and me in the governess cart. darcy dog sits up proud, her black coat splashed with a bib of white. harlequin the pony is really stepping out on the road to dimock's cote. a man in a big motor slows down *how much?* he calls to mum *i'll buy the whole outfit, how much?* the way he says *outfit* sounds like we've just been lifted from a box. harlequin raises his tail and green droppings tumble onto the road. *not for sale* mum says. the man curls his bottom lip, frowns a mock frown as he drives off, like he's been done out of his last sweetie

the way us fifth-form girls fell, we went down like piles of potatoes. my aunt called them *boy racers* as all they did was ride around in cars circling the school, and they kept driving, those boys rode us into lay-bys and lanes, abandoned us when we gave out.

'cos it was tina's second she was sent to live with fosterers down london way, came back with scars like red worms on her throat and arms, told me *don't let anything you can't name slip inside you at night and if it does, remember in the end it's not the falling that will finish you*

at dusk, we couldn't shut them all away. there were too many chickens to catch: rhode island reds and bantams and orpingtons, and all their mongrel chicks. they fluttered in the breeze like papers from next door's tip.

mum says i used to push them around the yard in my rusted silver cross pram. we gave them names: molly, daisy, flossie, daphne, meg, robert and the bossy margaret hatcher

i found molly by the rabbit hutches, mauled. but i learned: nothing is that lost it can't be killed again the following night

brace rigs an old shop bell behind his headboard on a
stretch of baler twine. it reaches out the window over the
gate and into the yard, where he ties a dead chicken called
molly to the other end and waits until night, his twelve-
bore by his side. i'm woken in the dark hours thinking
i've been hit around the head, but it's the sound of the
rifle gone off in the bedroom next to mine. in my ears
the whistling doesn't fade. *it was all over by the time
you heard it*, mum tells me the next day, but that night
there's a second shot. the night carries itself in on charcoal
legs, grinning teeth. i wet the bed and my body wears the
stench of those dead fox nights to school

some days, brace strings the foxes up on the walnut tree, their red coats much browner than i'd imagined, darker than the red paint chucked on our fence, but he's not angry. he smirks at *the townies*. other times, he piles foxes in the back of his motor to take to town, where he sells them at the back door of a restaurant. now i understand his laughter. i ask him the name of the place, but he revs away to buy more cartridges

the livestock dealers

we journeyed to cattle markets all over
but there was no way out of that house

where he made me watch him grope her
& i sat in the girl of my body

a squatter in someone else's story
dorothy gale on her yellow brick path

all those twists and turns
a hologram man at journey's end

sometimes i woke stretched across the back seat
a taste of fried onions in my mouth

and in the front, the radio blared *abilene, abilene*
prettiest town i've ever seen

and i became that place in the far-off
nobody ever reached

When I Talk About Codes

I go by three main definitions:
something converted into code to convey a secret meaning
something expressed in an indirect way
something assigned a code for purposes of classification or
identification.

The word *code* has its origins in a collection of Justinian statutes.
In school, I didn't question the prevailing view of the
Roman Empire in Britain.

> That it brought *civilisation* to the *peasants*.

In The Fens, people who resisted the invasion were known
thereafter as *brutish.*

> Boudicca was forced to watch her daughters being raped by
Roman soldiers.

There are two codes at the top of my medical record.
I see them each time I order a prescription.
These codes are immediately followed by their explanations:
X767N rape and *XaEFu physical abuse.*
This undermines the idea of codes as *secret* or *indirect*.

During my rape, the door was locked from the inside.
I said *No* three times. I heard small children outside.
My ears clutched their voices as a quilt against his rage.
The wall had begun to lose its afternoon light.

Somewhere a girl would be waiting for her mother
in the school playground. Thinking she'd been *forgotten*
(from the Old English *lose one's grip on*).
As in, I can't forget his hands around my throat.

I don't know who assigned codes *X767N* and *XaEFu*.
For many years I was unaware what they meant.

My rapist was someone I knew.
He doesn't have a criminal record code:
X767N rape is an indictable-only offence.

Meaning it must be tried in the Crown Court.
Meaning it's harder to get the crime heard.
Meaning the Crime Prosecution Service is more likely to throw it out.

A detective phoned to say the CPS would not proceed with my case.
After the rape, I had to prove physical resistance, a lack of consent.
Code *XaEFu physical abuse* was insufficient.

When I talk about codes, I'm aware of the successes and
failures of Justinian legacy.

there were times i wanted to destroy myself

down there
the place where all beginnings are made
                              there
where my daughters came from
the place their daughters will come from

abilene reads about the must farm man

in the newspaper, must farm man appears to smile
two rows of fine white teeth
though his face has almost dissolved
the vulnerability of his bones makes me cry
he's crouched in what the archaeologist terms *deepland*
so called for what the fen lacks in skyline
it makes up in beds of wet earth
with their scent of elderberry
sometimes it takes four thousand years
to reach the deepest layers of sod and loam
and expose the way-down dark

                              this is how it was
                  i wanted only to curl in on myself
                              an ammonite in dust
            left to slumber in blankets of dry peat
                            roots threaded between
                          my ribs, fingers and toes

abilene

dear john

a rat in the wheelie bin moment
                          that morning you called me
when i thought this is all
                  a piece of trash
dream a jacked-up johnny dream
                  i felt like a bottle thrown from a bridge
and somehow we were in it together
                  a ship, no captain and a vomit green sea

my name is abilene

i wear fluorescent nightclothes
and i want you to find me
crouched in the dark corner
of a derelict boathouse after a storm
      i believe in the sadness of rivers
sluiced off from their own mouths
at the widest part of their throats
how the ouse crawls towards the ocean
a river on its knees
      i don't forgive the water authority
for the protection it gives small flatlandish towns
there was a time i wished to slip beneath a steady current
and saucer down to the mud, a dead bivalve
my pearly insides full of slow decay
now all i want is a biblical flood
to take out those foggy lay-bys
          and their osseous branches
          that scratched at your car windows
      for all the nectarines of summer
          to be swept away
          with our scummy picnic blanket
      for the earrings necklaces bracelets rings
          you should never have bought me
          to become a child's treasure
          on that other-side-of-the-ocean beach
      for that cottage you live in with her
          and the carport you built
          on its spindly legs

to capsize and drift away like a ghost ship
marital and bloated with rot
my name is abilene
and i wear fluorescent nightclothes
i want you to find me
crouched in the dark

abilene spreads manure on her roses
while listening to power ballads

it was a resplendent spring john
as i laid it on thick john

at the roots of darcey bussell john
and precious time john

how the globules of horse manure shone john
like half-sunk pearls john

my girls felt all that warm decomposition john
rushin' rushin' inside john

their roots entwined and divine john
even when the neighbours complained john

about the manure and ammonia john
the round-the-clock stench and leakages john

the scraping fork of late-night fervour john
my girls wallowing in the slurry of my love john

and i turned up the volume john
to everything i do i do it for you john

until we ended john
my pretty flowers all in a fucking row john

the roses grew sick john
their passion seeped across the maize fields john

and into the ditches john
from where i filled my apothecary bottles john

to dab on your pillow each evening john
always your undying arable-defying maid john

what john said

i don't like kindness from women
it's too considerate
uncalled for
like warming the plate
before you hurl it at the door
i've just walked out of

as a boy the bruises on my arms
didn't give themselves up easily
five days of black and violet
two weeks of yellow

my mother had a millefiori paperweight
i carry its impact
at the corner of my lip
where it dozes
like a shiny bloodsucker

after we'd made love i told abilene
i slept with my ex last week

that's okay abilene said
everyone deserves a mercy fuck
i laughed for several seconds

until abilene replied
i was talking about you

john calls abilene *dramatic*

in response i bought us tickets to the jubilee
it was a joke that landed well
as john pulled me into the rhythms of the theatre bar
and staff in white shirts sloshed drinks onto a marble counter
i followed him through jackets and dresses
smothered by angora, scratched by denim
while the gluey floor sucked at my ballet flats
until we reached the carpeted stalls
where for a couple of hours we sat
and accepted the hero's poor judgements
knocked them back with too-sweet wine from plastic beakers

then john pretended to know when to laugh
the narrow seat restrained his movements
until he looked like a dangerous robot
which made me laugh
when there wasn't really much to laugh at
because the entire plot reminded me of my mum
who waited years for a thin band of gold

the lead actress knelt on the plastic grass
in front of an ivy-swaddled headstone
and i asked myself quietly
but ever so directly
what kind of woman kneels before such neglect?

abilene and the chesterfield

while loretta was away for the weekend
abilene brought john to her house
they sat on loretta's chesterfield
and john said *it's okay babe no one's guessed it's you*
the guys at work made a list of women
you didn't even make the top three

abilene got up and stared
at all those folds in the practical beige
pocked and criss-crossed
like constellation lines
branching into flanks and hocks
hard to believe this ghoulish piece of furniture
was once an animal with heart-chambers
bull's blood pumping through its veins

a road sweeper saves abilene's life

when the heart-to-heart you offer me in this metal-
framed bed is a disservice to hearts everywhere, john,
i offer up my love to the early morning road-sweeper
on his seventh or eighth pass by this airbnb window.
skimming the hungover pavement, he offers me a
new language. he whirs the weight of the night in my
ears, over crossroads and bridges, never reaching the
distance for a complete fade-out

john, you were my revolutionary, but now my ears
want nothing but road-sweeper purr. the judder of a
hundred tanks couldn't outdo it, that steadfast road-
sweeper courage

the lamppost that held its yellow beam over me all night
may be callous or desperate, or perhaps a grieving moon
fit only for ornamental purposes. the window-frame
sectioned its light into eight squares, shone it onto the
floor, made me want to jump onto each reflected pane,
stamp out the brightness

in the language of paving-stones i tell you goodbye.
in the dialect of a hundred tanks i tell you goodbye.
john, a road-sweeper is dancing my heart away, while
the night holds its yellow beam over me. the bridges
are desperate, our bed is a grieving ornament, the
revolution is off

too late abilene

instead of him, i dial men i've met briefly
at parties or friend's houses
can't even remember
why i have their numbers
i drift off to their words

. . . cold front coming . . . next week is good . . .
clean out the gutters . . . when i get back from . . .
put up those fence panels . . . all out of date

clod frnot cmonig . . . nxet weke is doog . . .
cealn uot the gtuters . . . wehn i gte bcak form
ptu up tohse fncee paenls all uot of dtae

little boy, i'm deboned by the thought
that you'll be innuendoed by the prussian

with her ribboned stockings and bedside toddy
please understand this, when you kiss her

under a snooded moon on basin street
wearing boonie shoes and a sodden suede coat

i won't be sky-thinking
i'll be nose-diving

in denial with something borrowed
from cowgirls and mischief-makers

and distracted in my bed, i'll slowly fillet
each white rib from my corset

too late abilene
too late

abilene canvassing in windmill gardens

there are so many ways to create disorder in a cul-de-sac
while wearing a shiny rosette, as i cut corners and walk
over zones of lawn and ornamental slate. i brush against
reversed-in citroëns and kias. i set off a bedlam of lights
and am scolded by the *bweep bweep bweep* of alarms

with its repurposed wheelbarrows full of hydrangeas and
hostas, this development is container-gardening at its
miracle-gro finest. no loungers or bare soil showing

in the pale-stone patio years of my life, john, i want to live
with you in windmill gardens. i want to spill châteauneuf-
du-pape on our rattan chairs. i want us to come to harm
by gnat and devilled egg beneath the visible filaments in
our festoon lighting. i want to go to the penny peg garden
center and look at pergolas with you, keeping quiet when
you insist it's *pagoda*

john, i keep going down dead-ends off dead-ends, all the
musical doorbells are playing *the yellow rose of texas*. i
tap a rhythm of *shave and a haircut, two bits* on the brass
knockers. the dahlia heads are nodding, but you're not
answering, john. john?

abilene running around solarcity

the laugh out loud part
wasn't that i'd gotten myself lost
it was my search for a landmark
in two hundred acres of solar panels
where milk-white sheep busied
their masked faces with roughage

i blame you, john
you hadn't called for days
but the glint and glare of fifty megawatts
from all the panels on the old furze fields
began to make me feel alive, john
just parked there sunning themselves
their faces turned to heaven
with thanks for their big-tech shine

nerdy things, john
how they'll never know
what it feels like to be run out of yourself
searching for something
and going against the advice
when lost just stay in one place

abilene wears a lipstick called *rouge 999*

in the home-streaming version
though the air is filled with rot
my negligee sticky with flies
this is a world in which mascara never smudges,
not even when i'm dredged from my bed
a rim of muck on my once-pedicured nails
for months i've slopped about
and dreamt of you john
willed my lips to become your emergency

nothing really severs

i ask google if he'll contact me again
            a voice crackles like a bad hook-up
      how do you know if anyone's listening?
      how do you know if anyone's listening?
zari ballard is listening
she reminds me of all those 2am awakenings
      the unreceived texts

my bedroom is wallpapered in zari
LOVE DOESN'T DIE A NATURAL DEATH
LOVE HAS TO BE KILLED

        zari tells me
        we can walk away
        run away
        stop answering the phone
        delete the texts
        block his emails
        we know all that

        and most of us even do all that
        but nothing really severs

i didn't see the ending
so much as feel the static of it
as the sky lost itself
in fierce *please leave pink*

the holiday let
seven nights of board games

how the snakes always look so glam
draped across the squares

the blue and yellow diamonds on their backs glint
climb on for a ride

the plain wooden ladders
utilitarian yet not

going nowhere near any kind of sky
there's a reason they share a board

snake and ladder
both caught up with waiting

for whatever consequence
the dice is going to chuck at them

❧

we used to lie on starched white sheets and dig into the
low-grade soil of ourselves. he told me that growing up
he ate chips every day. i told him when i had an eating
disorder, i didn't eat potatoes for ten years. he told me at
his heaviest, he weighed three times my lightest weight

i plant myself in a clunchy field
let my eyes stop working as eyes
the quality of the soil is less important
than the ability to make myself
as unalive as possible

on wild days i snuggle up with vermin skulls
thread my hair through their sockets
he might dig me up sometime
my skin powdering his hands
like a terrifying fossil

when you buy a potato it's still living
no heart no pulse but all of its potato
family instinctively know it as a conscious being
she asks how i'm getting on
and i say *like a potato, sis,*
like a potato

it's never my successfully-in-love friends
who are posting motivational crap on insta
nevertheless when daniel tells me
i shouldn't use the word *try*
but instead should say *i am*
moving on i forgive him

i *yay!* enthusiasm at his grindr pic
eat the cheese and tomato sandwiches
daniel has buttered and sliced
drink pomegranate juice
try to make myself new

                    thirty years from now
          we'll sit in daniel's electric volvo
        face an escarpment of ancient coast
              blurred by summer rain

                    we'll eat fish and chips
    as he points to where the sea once rolled in

his name was mike

i thought he might erase john

his warmth and weight double

and after

i even laid my head on his shoulder

leant into its sturdiness

for a minute

when bored i think of ways i might ruin his life
not john but the man who sent me messages
every week through my website
requested my online friends
snatched a photo of me
in a red bikini on a beach
happy new year scrawled across my tummy
sent my photo to john
told him *we're in a relationship*
a part of john wanted to believe him
he'd seen his strava how it detailed him
running past my house in the early hours
eight times in two weeks
but *it's not enough* the police said
to be classed as stalking

abecedarian for the vagina

after him, i just want to own myself again
but some days i imagine his residue
casually lolling about inside me
daubed on my cervix like ghost slime
every vagina he touched is probably googling its future self –
fanny fix, genital aesthetic surgery, labiaplasty, cosmetic gynaecology
gucci cucci. my friend kim laughs
how i'd have to save for eighteen months just to be scraped
i should ask him to pay for it
just a little re-texturising
kim says her ex told her she was *too fleshy*
like skate wings – as if
male genitals should be large and prominent and female genitals as lack
no one wants chopped liver between her legs, he told her, *you need to*
offer it up smooth
oyster on the half-shell, kim and i call our cunts posh names
pudendum, she says, *that high falutin' word comes from the latin for*
shame
quim, i say, my gran said it with such gusto she made it sound like a
restorative drink
reject all who tell you the new vag is just the same old pussy having shed
its winter coat
sphynx vs angora because all men want in life is a bald kitty
tautness is the hymen re-attached option with botox as an additional
extra, a brochure reads
upstream from the beaver family then, i say
victoria, kim gives her imaginary new vag a name
when i'm out with victoria, i'll feel like the queen of sheba
xerical references are not ideal, we laugh

you ever wonder what'd happen if we stopped looking at
                                    ourselves through a man's mirror? kim asks
zero men, their mirrors, their cum shifting inside us like plankton

what john told people about abilene

she comes from the boglands / lights fires in neighbour's
gardens / dances naked widdershins around the church / is
the daughter of a belgian / has a witch's mark on her / hides
her tail beneath long skirts / speaks in tongues / smokes a
pipe / is five hundred years old / drinks sap from deadly
nightshade / eats pies made of sparrows / shapeshifts into a
bat / has no heart / has an extra nipple / bleeds green every
month / cut away her own hymen and buried it under a
yew tree / holds a silver mirror between her legs to reflect
the red flesh burning in the morning sky / that she loved
him like no other

well fyt john because i'm hanging with rexie again

as a teen rexie taught me to walk on black ice
in white stilettos
a mile-and-a-half home from the chequers
keep your back straight and relaxed
half a calorie a step
rexie said the *clink clink* of my heels
sounded like a caviar spoon against glass
she had an ear for offenbach
and an eye for america in neon
all that steel all those angles
19-year-old kate moss on broadway
posing like a god
those nights rexie held me until i was warm
you've got to commit she whispered
i clipped-in to the pedals of the bike rexie lent me
and cycled against the wind
on the days when i couldn't get out of bed
rexie pressed hot stones into the hollows
beneath my shoulders and ribcage
she traced my lips with her finger
and told me i was *à la mode*
by dusk a handful of rexie's plastic-coated pills
jewelled the depths of my stomach
how they disappeared like beautiful girls
locked in a basement

14 ways to deal with nostalgia

if it turns up without top shelf wine don't let it sit at the table
stack the blue and white dinner plates
put the engraved silverware back in the drawer
snuff out the candles
pause elvis costello
feed the cat for a second time
consider moving to bury st edmunds
find your longline m&s cardigan
climb the only hill you can find in the fens
sit in the clover with slow-moving bumblebees
look down on fields being swallowed by big machinery
chew a blade of grass
try to remember a line by john clare
try to remember a line by john clare

in the town of the gaslit women

when we call for the men who installed us here
we do so in the dialect of primrose or hollyhock

yet to speak their names is to sift
syllables through gravel

while we wait we beat a soulful rhythm
with our ringless fingers

that could be dorset rain on shingle
or on any beach of promises we can't forget

but the roads out of town hiss and froth
until the image of a woman hangs monstrous above

only then do we shake out our memories –
a bouquet of dry flowers in the breeze

as none of us wants to be her
not again

probable grizzly bear attack

john you've given me a gift
in the way that details might save me
the claw marks on my back door
all those overturned bins
the fur snagged on my fence

i keep going up and down my road
past the neighbour's swaggering buddleia
the same raised paving slabs
but i can't find it
wherever it is i think it's yours john
please look after your bear

fluffy toy dog

someone gave you to me john
like a fluffy toy dog
you sat eagerly on my bed
awaiting my attention
but your obscene furriness
was thick with grime from other sheets

everyone's version of heaven is different

i've given up self-medicating
with fluffy toy dogs
and texts from sermonising men
who tell me the average person speaks
eleven million words a year
there isn't really an average though
it's their way of saying give me some
or three of your eleven million

just think by the time we reach our forties
the world's got a couple of decades of xanax behind it
slumped in the corner with its hands over its ears
the world's like any parent at the end of a village-hall party
burping up funfetti cupcakes
it's not the world's fault we all do it
trying to recapture sweet encounters
alice is still smooshing cake into phoebe's hair
and jj's throwing wet toilet roll against the wall

all i truly want is the snake
to offer me his version of paradise
with fake white sand
a couple of scratchy loungers
and those big red apples on the breakfast bar
not a hint of flavour in them
but how they make me want to eat and eat

abilene's head is a fairground

the galloping horses are back
impaled on glossy poles
all they do is carousel round and round
a damp room with plastic-backed curtains
flanks glassy and cold as cockroach shells

nights like these need a soundtrack
of wheezy barrel organs and hurdy gurdies
a grinning percussion monkey
a drum-tap of hooves on never-ending legs

these horses wear scrolls around their necks
red on gold lettering: *abilene* and *john*
at first they appear on the same rotation
then judder to a stop at six and twelve

it's a strange light this evening

dear john my scars are ghost-white and meshed like antique lace i want to take the scissors to them / dear abilene such savagery in the breeze tonight / dear john my hair is blown around my ears like cornsilk my neck readied for the blade / dear abilene it's a strange light this evening / dear john after we parted the garden shrieked and fanned its plumage into finger-like protuberances / dear abilene every day i hope the earth spits you out like a worm / dear john things thrown up from the land are just eager to see the morning sun / dear abilene you burrow inside me like a splinter / dear john after i left you my bones began to glow zinc white and pearl / dear abilene what a stunning canvas / dear john did you ever return to the abbey and take her with you? / dear abilene the water in the well has turned to coin / dear john i have lost count of my wishes / dear abilene how many wishes were in the bag you picked up when you walked past my kiss? / dear john do you mean the kiss you saved for her?

the hammer and the vase

i saw a soft-faced hammer
in the tools section of jackson's
just as a song announced itself
over the radio and in the way
i'd forgotten eighties frozen desserts
until this morning, i'd stopped thinking about this song
it tempted me like viennetta
made me want to sit on the icy tiles
with a bowl and a spoon
such a distraction from the soft-faced hammer
that looked so clean-living when hanging
beside the claws and ball-peins and clubs
precision without damage
in the softness of a soft-faced hammer
it had aesthetic purpose
but the song sent me back home
where the effort of crying
filled five small vases of corncockle and buttercups
and a notebook where i wrote
the morning hit me like a club
hanging in the tools section of jackson's
with a bowl and a spoon
and there was an eighties frozen dessert
announcing itself over the radio
crying felt so clean-living when sitting
beside the claws and ball-peins and clubs
and the white tile floor had aesthetic purpose
the soft-faced hammer made me want to go home
fill a small vase with tears

and place it on the bottom stair
you be the hammer and i'll be the vase, john
let's be those things for each other

it's about a small plot of land

john, we fen dwellers are what savage minds make us
according to the broadcaster and the entertainer
you used to listen to on weekday mornings
how he created a fictional fenman
who lived in a railway carriage on a small plot of land
with his elderly mother and played the banjo
how the term *fen hovel wife* was never questioned
how banjo playing in the fens was never questioned
i always felt uneasy the broadcaster said
in making his imaginary fen village *so squalid*
hopeless and all round awful
but i blame the public – savage is what they wanted
but now, john, they're not so sure

i sit in a hardback chair and listen to storm warnings

there's a basket in the corner of the room
filled with all our lost and broken parts
a reel of medical tape
a chipped beach pebble
a single ticket to a stoppard play
a nail lacquer called *into the night*
a postcard of degas's *girl dancer at the barre*
a ceramic unicorn in rainbow colours
and a pinecone closed for rain
i pick nothing but the radio
tonight it calls my name
something not quite song
not quite prayer
its music sending messages
from one village to the next
how do you choose which possessions to take?

relic

i light a candle in the empty chapel
john doesn't hear me
but the saint does
there's a smear of ash on the glass
as the curtain is pulled back
how did your skin get so grey?
many flames many flames she tells me
her thumb is bowed like a spur
how did your flesh become so thickened?
much praying much praying
her palm is yellow
textured like an eel's underside
and your fingers grow so long?
much binding and loosing
binding and loosing
there's a small rust-coloured stain
on the silk pillow that cushions her wrist
how did your body go astray?
many stones many stones

Your Receipt

Post Office Ltd.

        Addressee:
        John,
        an east-coast-ghost, years away
        from the gnarled plastic chairs
        in my freezing waiting room

Item Price	Total
Inc. VAT	

Rogue expectation months

7	@	1.00	7.00	=

    Days are best met without a mirror

Woman running

1	@	1.00	1.00	=

    How my ghost submits to a weigh-in

Recipe Books

2	@	1.00	2.00	=

    and you're telling people I'm boiling my pot . . .

Charles Shaw wine bottles

8	@	1.00	8.00	=

    I drink myself empty

The zigzags of my midriff

2   @   1.00   2.00   =

Denim's safest when expandable

A thick comforter on the bed

1   @   1.00   1.00   =

My body in a sealed-up hug

Dating apps

4   @   1.00   4.00   =

How to muffle the yob-calls of my fem parts

A cold spring

1   @   1.00   1.00   =

The doorless igloo as state of mind

A warm summer's day

1   @   1.00   1.00   =

One fizzing fly on life's carcass

The menace of a parcel

1   @   1.00   1.00   =

Parts of me just want to be in touch

Total   =   a petrified exit (un)strategy

Please retain for future reference.
Thank you.

Thanks and Acknowledgements

'hanging with rexie', shortlisted for the *Ambit* competition, 2021, and published in *Ambit*.

'paradise farm', published in *Ink, Sweat & Tears*, 2022.

'i wear a lipstick called rouge 999', longlisted in publisher the6ress's David Lynch-inspired competition and published in the *Invitation to Love* anthology, 2022.

An earlier version of 'bormed' was shortlisted for the *Aesthetica Magazine* International Poetry Prize, 2021 and published in the competition anthology. Also, longlisted for *The Rialto* Nature and Place Competition, 2020.

'everyone's version of heaven is different', published in *Ink, Sweat & Tears*, 2021 and voted as 'Pick of the Month.'

p.17 prose poem formerly titled 'if one of us forgets to water the flowers and herbs,' commended in the 2020 Café Writers' Competition, published on the Café Writers' website.

'the box of maternal recall', shortlisted for the 2020 Café Writers' Competition.

'14 ways to deal with nostalgia', published in *14 Magazine*, 2021

Selected poems commissioned by Blackfield Creatives' *You are Important Project*, 2022

'Your Receipt' published in *Magma 83, Solitude*

'my name is abilene' published in *Magma 83, Solitude*

Selected poems chosen for Nine Pens *Nine Series Anthologies*.

Huge thanks to the following poets who have read the manuscript or seen earlier versions of the poems in *my name is abilene*: Sharon Black, Rebecca Goss, Rachael Allen, Daljit Nagra, Maurice Riordan, Richard Scott, Julia Webb, Alice Frecknell, Toby Campion, Cecilia Knapp, Bryony Littlefair, Maria Ferguson, Talia Randall and John Greening. Enormous gratitude to Chris and Jen Hamilton-Emery for taking on *abilene*.

This book has been typeset by
SALT PUBLISHING LIMITED
using Sabon, a font designed by Jan Tschichold
for the D. Stempel AG, Linotype and Monotype Foundries.
It is manufactured using Holmen Book Cream 65gsm,
a Forest Stewardship Council™ certified paper from the
Hallsta Paper Mill in Sweden. It was printed and bound
by Clays Limited in Bungay, Suffolk, Great Britain.

CROMER
GREAT BRITAIN
MMXXIII